Healing Images for Children

Activity Book

Coloring/Drawing/Playing/Writing

For Days When Quiet Activities are Best

Written by Nancy C. Klein
Illustrated by Matthew Holden

Published by Inner Coaching
Watertown, Wisconsin

Klein, Nancy C.
    Healing images for children activity book:
    For days when quiet activities are best / by
    Nancy C. Klein : illustrated by Matthew Holden.

    Activities that encourage self-expression,
    as well as self-help ideas for any child coping
    with illness or hospitalization.

    ISBN 0-9636027-4-8

Published by Inner Coaching
1108 Western Avenue
Watertown, Wisconsin 53094
(920) 262-0439

The material in this book is provided for educational and informational purposes only, and is not intended to be a substitute for medical advice. A physician or appropriate health care professional should always be consulted for any health or medical concerns.

Illustrated by Matthew Holden
Cover Design by Joel Richter
Interior Design by Nancy Klein

Printed in the United States of America

First Edition

About This Book

Children will find many hours of enjoyment within this book. The activities can be enjoyed at any time but they are especially good for quiet times such as waiting for appointments, driving in the car, and during times of rest and recuperation.

This book is much more than a coloring book.

Each page reinforces a positive statement. A main idea is suggested, but the pictures are designed to be open-ended. Children can bring their own ideas to the pages. The drawings allow children to develop and express personal interpretations of the positive statements. The goal is to reinforce the messages so your child is able to remember them and use them when needed in other situations. Your child's involvement promotes "learning by doing" which is an effective method for remembering important information.

In addition to the pictures, there are pages for writing about feelings and experiences. Games, mazes, and puzzles are also included. Several of the activities can be enjoyed with a friend. Individual activities are designed for several different levels of difficulty and will appeal to children ranging in age from approximately 4 to 12+ years old. Siblings who are experiencing many of the events in their brother or sister's life also enjoy having their own copy of the Activity Book.

These child-centered activities help reframe medical events so children are better able to cope with potential stress. Many of the pages have therapeutic applications that are described on the pages *For Parents and Therapists*.

The activities help children anchor the meaning of the active imagination stories and positive statements from the book, *Healing Images for Children -Teaching Relaxation and Guided Imagery to Children Facing Cancer and Other Serious Illnesses*. However, the *Activity Book* can be used independently from *Healing Images for Children*. Information about the *Healing Images for Children* resources can be found in the appendix.

My name is Bailey.

Dear Friend,

    I am the star of this book! You'll find me on most of the pages. I hope you enjoy coloring and playing games with me.

    Let me tell you a little bit about myself.   I love to be outside. I chase butterflies and squirrels. I dig in the dirt. I put my nose on the sidewalk and I follow ants. It's a pretty great life for a dog.

    I also love quiet times indoors. I curl up on the sofa and I take a nap. I lay around on my back with my feet up in the air and I take a nap. I chew on toys for awhile and then I nap. Wait a minute! I could use some more excitement when I'm inside. How about you? Do you ever have times when you're looking for something interesting to do?

    That's where this book comes in handy. It's filled with pictures to color, games to play with a friend, and pages for writing down your thoughts. It's a book that encourages you to use your imagination. It gives you positive messages about your life.

    Let's have fun! (And maybe then I'll take a nap!)

Sincerely,

Bailey

How to Draw Bailey

1.

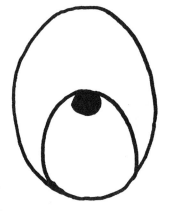

FIRST DRAW AN OVAL SHAPE WITH A BIG SPOT IN THE MIDDLE. THAT WILL BE THE TOP OF ANOTHER OVAL.

2.

NEXT DRAW A LITTLE SMILE HALF WAY DOWN FROM THE SPOT. THEN TWO MORE OVALS FOR THE EYES.

3.

NOW DRAW IN THE EYE BROWS, EARS, AND MUSTACHE. FINALLY, FINISH THE EYES. AFTER SOME PRACTICE, YOU CAN DRAW BAILEY ANY WHERE, WHENEVER YOU WANT!

Now You Try to Draw Bailey

This is me!

Draw a picture of yourself.

"My body is filled with healthy cells that heal me."

Make a picture of your body feeling healthy and strong.

Draw a picture of your pet or favorite animal.

These are Bailey's friends Shadow and Waldo.

These are my friends!

Draw a picture of something you like to do with your friends.

"I share my day with special people."

Think of all the ways that you can keep in touch with friends:
Visiting, calling on the phone, emailing, sending cards and letters, making
videos and tape recordings.

A Magical Dragon Friend

Pretend that you know a friendly dragon. You fly through the sky together and go on adventures. Color a picture of you and your dragon as the two of you travel through the air.

Friends are special. You can play with friends, laugh with friends, and share your feelings with friends. Imagine telling your dragon friend how you feel.
On each line think of something that begins with that letter.

Things that make me happy.

D_Dogs_____
R_____
A_delyn and Alyna___
G_riffin_____
O_____
N_____

Things that make me sad.

D_ogs ~~cat~~ Dieing__
R_____
A_____
G_____
O_____
N_____

Things that make me angry.

D_____
R_____
A_____
G_____
O_____
N_____

Things that make me peaceful.

D_____
R_oom_____
A_____
G_____
O_____
N_____

"It feels good to express my feelings."

You have many different emotions. You can express your feelings in ways that are safe and that help you feel better.

This is Bailey's house.

This is where I live!

Draw a picture of your house the way it looks in your favorite season.

A Special Treat for Bailey

Color by number. Choose 3 of your favorite colors.

Color # 1 _____

Color # 2 _____

Color # 3 _____

Fill in each space with the color that matches the number.

What is Bailey's yummy treat? _____

What is Bailey saying? _____

A Special Treat for You

Decorate your cake with your favorite colors and designs.

"I breathe in comfort and peace. I blow out difficulties and problems."

You can use your breath to pretend to blow out candles. Concentrating on your breathing can help distract you from uncomfortable feelings.

~ Relax Your Muscles ~
An active imagination "read-aloud" story

Pretend that you are sitting by a pond with your turtle friend next to you. It is a sunny day and you and your turtle friend are resting on a rock warmed by the sun. Take a deep breath. As you breathe out, stretch out your neck as far as you can, as if you were a turtle poking its head out of its shell. Hold the stretch as you count to three: 1 – 2 –3. Now relax and let the tightness flow out of your muscles. Let the stretch melt. Notice the soft, relaxed feeling in your face, neck, and shoulders. Continue to take gentle breaths, in and out.

Next, tighten your arms by bending your elbows and bringing your fists to your shoulders. Feel the tension and hold it as you count to three: 1 – 2 – 3. Release all the tightness from your hands, arms, back, and shoulders.

Now, tighten the muscles in your legs by keeping your legs straight and pulling your toes toward your chin. Hold the tightness as you count to three: 1 – 2 – 3. Now, relax the muscles in your legs. Feel the relaxation throughout your body.
Enjoy this feeling.

You and your turtle are ready to have a restful day together. It is fine to move slowly today and to be at peace. Your turtle knows how much energy you have and it knows you are moving at just the right pace for the way you feel today. You look forward to today's activities. You know you will enjoy your day.

The two of you slowly and patiently move to the edge of the rock. Imagine gently easing off the rock and gliding into the water. You feel light in the water.

Take some time to travel around the pond with your turtle. Say hello to the birds you meet as they build their nests. Swim past frogs sitting on lily pads. Dive under the surface of the water and visit the beavers building their lodge. Everyone is glad to see you. There is much to see and appreciate. There is life all around you.

Say to yourself three times: **"I am strong and I have energy to enjoy my day."** As you swim through the warm water, feel it glide over your body. Paddle gently through the water and enjoy the feeling.

When you feel ready, head back to your rock. Slip out of the water and climb onto your special place, a place where you can sit in the sun and enjoy the day.

Whenever you want to help yourself feel calm and relaxed, think about slow, gentle breathing, tightening then relaxing muscles, gently floating in the water, and greeting the animals in the pond as you did in this story.

Find the Matching Designs

As you color the turtle's shell look for the swirls that match each other and draw a line to connect them.

"I am strong and I have energy to enjoy my day."

MY PHOTO ALBUM
OF MY
ADVENTURES WITH TURTLE

Color pictures to show adventures that you could have
with your turtle friend.

Bailey wonders . . .

Take a few minutes each day to tell Bailey how you are feeling and what you are thinking about. You can start by writing, drawing, or telling someone your answers to these questions.

How do you feel today?

What would make you feel better?

Tell me about your day.

What do you have planned for your day?

Who did you talk to today?

Did you learn any new tricks today?

Tell me about things that you enjoy doing.

Find the Hidden Fish

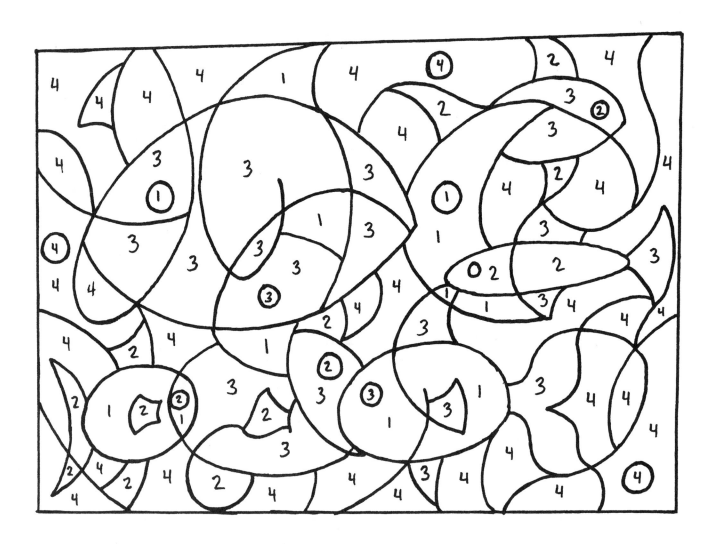

Color by number. Choose 4 beautiful colors and fill in the spaces
in the picture that go with each number.

Color # 1 _____

Color # 2 _____

Color # 3 _____

Color # 4 _____

How many fish can you see? _____

While You Are Waiting

Make a picture of an aquarium and fill it with interesting things.

An active imagination "read-aloud" story
Take time to relax your muscles and take calm, peaceful breaths.

When you are sitting in a waiting room use your imagination and think about a large aquarium. Pretend that you, and all the other people who are in the waiting room, are beautiful tropical fish swimming in this large fish tank. Imagine that the clothes the people are wearing are actually their colorful scales.

Look around at all the other fish people. Big fish, little fish. Each one is beautiful in the water. Some are rushing past. Some move slowly. Some are sitting quietly and watching the others. Some are talking to each other. Each one is different and is here for a different reason. You are happy to have some extra time to observe the gentle movement of people around you.

You feel relaxed about being in the waiting room today. You are here for an important reason. You know that people are in waiting rooms for all different reasons. Say to yourself three times, **"My day is filled with interesting people."**

Using your imagination to think about interesting things helps the waiting time pass quickly and helps you feel calm.

Help the dolphin find the path that leads to the bottom of the ocean.

Explore the Ocean with a Dolphin

Color a picture of the underwater scene that the two of you discover.

"I have a calm, pain free place I can go to."

Sometimes you might want to find a shady, cool, quiet spot to rest. Pretend to swim like dolphins do, exploring the ocean and then coming up to breathe. The gentle movement of swimming and the cool water comforts you.

Up, Up, and Away

Color a design on the hot air balloon. Draw what you see when you look up at the clouds. Draw what you see on the ground. Draw people in the basket that are going on the trip with you.

"My body feels comfortable and at peace."

On an imaginary ride in a hot air balloon you can think about rising above sensations of pain or discomfort. Concentrate on picturing yourself being comfortable as you fly high above any problems or worries.

What's Up?

The giraffe has a long, strong neck. Add a pleasant, happy, positive word or thought to some spots on the giraffe's neck. If you can't fill in the spots right away, that's okay. Take your time. Wait for another day.

"Good things will come."

Design Your Dream Playground

What would be on your dream playground? Color a picture with all the great toys and equipment that you would include.

Draw the scene that you see when you are at the top of the slide.

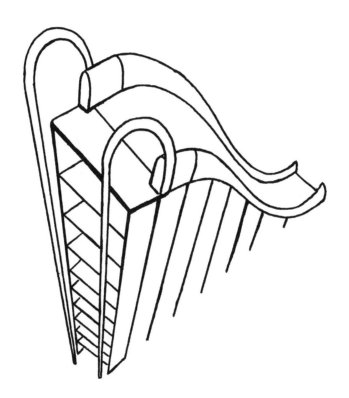

"I climb up to good feelings."

Use your imagination to climb above painful sensations when you want to feel more comfortable. Pretend to drop unwanted feelings off the top of the slide and imagine them sinking deep into the ground.

A Colorful Field of Flowers

Your garden attracts butterflies and bumblebees. Birds visit.
Insects crawl among the plants. It is a place full of life and
beauty.

"I am able to make myself feel comfortable."

Sometimes you have an experience that is uncomfortable. It is possible to
lessen uncomfortable sensations by using your mind and imagination to focus
on other feelings. Think about the colors of butterflies, the sounds of
nature, and the smells of flowers to help yourself feel comfortable.

MY JOURNAL

You have many important ideas and feelings.
You can let others know what you are thinking about by talking,
writing, and drawing your ideas.
Use words and/or pictures to express your opinions on these
pages.

My favorite lunch is...

I have fun when I spend time with...

I like to read about...

Today I want to...

Today I learned about...

When it is cold I like to...

The TV show I like best is...

It makes me angry when...

My birthday is...

This summer I want to...

I love...

My favorite animal is...

When it is hot I like to...

I feel confused about...

I want to take a trip to...

I worry about...

I sometimes wonder...

Someone I admire is...

3 things that make me happy are...

I do not like...

3 things that make me sad are...

I am thankful for...

The color I like best is...

Today I feel...

I wish for...

I like to play...

My best toy is...

Crossword Puzzle

The pictures are your clues. Fit the words into the boxes.

Bailey   bone   giraffe   tree   turtle

Hospital bracelets list important information about people.

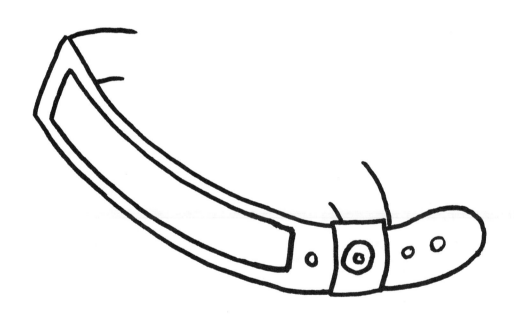

Put your left wrist over the bracelet and then trace your hand on the page.
Write a message on the bracelet that tells something important about you.

It's Nice to Meet You

You meet many people at a hospital doing important jobs that help others become healthier. Draw pictures of the new people you meet.

"Everyone is working together to help me."

My Future's So Bright ......

Design a pair of sunglasses that let you look at the world in a new way. Pretend to wear your imaginary sunglasses when you meet new people and go to new places.

"I feel confident and calm in new experiences and new places."

When you go to new places you discover new sights, new sounds, new smells, and you often meet new people. There is much to do and to learn in our world.

Bailey's Amazing Adventure

Can you travel with Bailey to find the path that leads from the parking lot to the doctor's office?

Start your trip at the parking lot.

Stop at the lab for a blood test.

LAB

X-Ray Department. Time for a peek inside.

Cafeteria. Bailey wants a snack.

Waiting Room. Play a game together.

Doctor's Office. You made it to your appointment!

Bailey, Shadow, Waldo, and Sammy had x-rays taken. Draw lines to help the doctor match each dog to the correct x-ray. Then color the dogs.

Design a Flag

Make pictures on your flag that show you feeling happy, healthy, and strong.

"I am happy, healthy, and strong."

If you have a spot inside your body that hurts, use your imagination to mark it with a flag. Focus your attention only on the movement of the flag and you will be distracted from the uncomfortable feeling.

Putting Out Fires

Start at the hydrant and follow the path of each hose. Use a different color each time.

"The medicine I take helps my body heal."

Imagine being a firefighter who sprays water on a fire to put it out. Now think about your medicine going through your body and putting out unhealthy cells and germs. Your medicine makes you healthier and more comfortable.

A Sparkling Celebration

Imagine a night sky filled with the sparkling colors of fireworks!
You can create a picture of fireworks lighting up the sky.
Here's how to do it.

First, use crayons and fill the whole frame with patches of different colors. Press hard.

Next, cover everything with your black crayon.

Now you are ready to make the fireworks. Using a pencil, press lightly and scratch off the top layer of black crayon. The colors underneath will show as you create your fireworks designs.

"My healthy cells take charge."

Imagine a celebration inside your body as mixed-up cells and germs are destroyed by your immune system, your medicine, and your treatments.

Using the letters in
Arcade Game
how many new words
can you spell?
Fill the screen with
the words you make.

"Unhealthy cells are easy targets."

What Does Not Belong in this Picture?
As you color the picture circle all the mixed-up things.

Follow the Lines

Color each bag of medicine a different color. Follow each tube into the body until the medicine reaches the mixed-up cells.

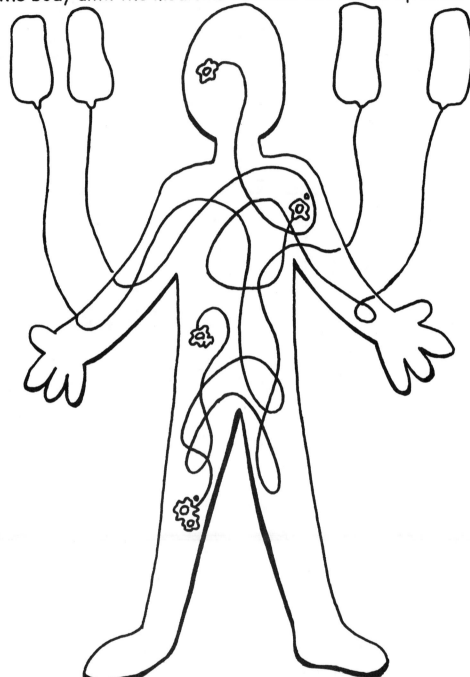

"The medicine I take brightens my body with healing."

Taking medicine is part of getting healthier and feeling better. Doctors prescribe medicine to fight disease and to calm pain.

Giggle Wiggles

Here's a way to have some fun, alone or with a friend.
Make a little wiggly line somewhere on the paper.
Use your imagination to turn the line into a picture.
Take turns. Ask your friend to make a line for you, then you
make one for your buddy. Have fun!

Be creative in the way you look at your world. We all see
things in our own way. You are unique.

Color a Rainbow

After a rainstorm you can
sometimes see a rainbow in the sky.

Follow the Rainbow

If you discovered a treasure at the end of the rainbow what would it be? Color a picture of your treasure.

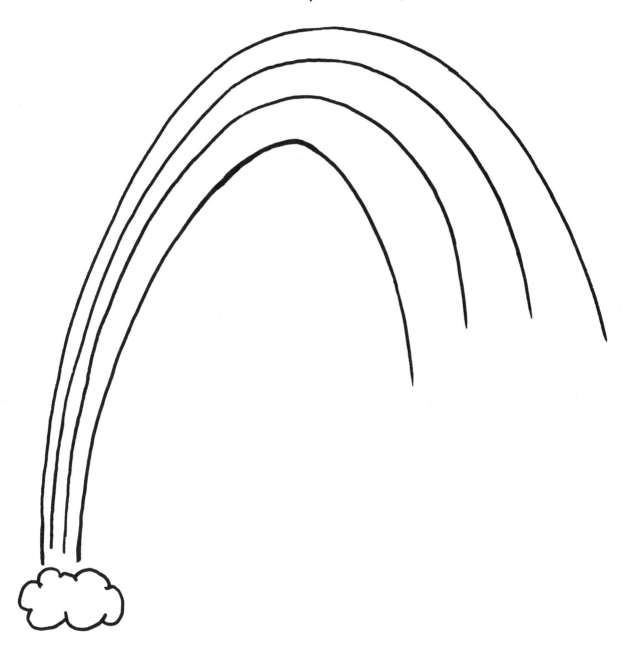

"I discover treasures in my life."

The special treasures in our lives are not always "things." Sometimes they are people, places, memories, and our dreams.

Rainbow Treats

Think of your favorite foods that match each
of the colors.

Red _____

Orange _____

Yellow _____

Green _____

Blue _____

Purple _____

"The medicine I take brightens my body with healing."

Think about swallowing these delicious tastes to make a rainbow inside your
body. Follow the rainbow with your medicine. When you take your medicine
think of it joining the rainbow inside your body. Your body is filled with good
flavors.

Discover the Secret Message

CROSS OUT THE LETTERS B C M P W Z EACH TIME THEY APPEAR.

N E Z C V E R B F M O
R G E W T P C T O E P
Z A T W B H E A L C Z
T H Y M P F O B O D P S

FILL IN THE REMAINING LETTERS IN THE BLANK SPACES BELOW.
P.S.   GOOD LUCK!

* *

— — — — —   — — — — — —

— —   — — —

— — — — — — —

— — — — — — !

"I make healthy choices."

Sometimes an illness or a medicine may change our appetite. If that
happens we can carefully choose foods that help our bodies feel better.

Let the Stars Shine

Let the stars in the sky remind you of each of the people who love you and who take care of you.

"I am loved and cared for."

Add stars to the sky for the special people in your life.

Pleasant Dreams

Think about something special that has happened to you.

"I dream happy dreams."

Thinking pleasant thoughts can help you relax and feel ready for sleep.

Star Light – Star Bright. . .
First star I see tonight, I wish I may, I wish I might,
Have this wish I wish tonight.

Make a wish. Color a picture of your wish coming true.

"I have a special wish."

When you wish something and
think about doing it, it helps you
plan for the future. Make a list
of the things you can do to make
your wish come true.

Blast Off!

Draw your face in the spaceship window.
Color the scenes you see as you travel through outer space.

"My stomach stays calm and steady."

Sometimes stomachs feel queasy. If your stomach is upset, pretend that you can travel on a smooth, peaceful flight into outer space. Thinking about your trip will help you keep a calm feeling in your stomach.

The Settlers

Connect the dots to discover what you are traveling in on this trip across the prairie.

Draw Your Smooth, Steady Path

Color the things you see along the trail.

"As I relax, my stomach settles down."

Imagine taking a relaxing trip on a trail that is straight and smooth. Watch the eagles fly. Picture the grasses and flowers waving gently as you travel. These thoughts help your stomach stay calm.

CROSSWORD PUZZLE CLUES

ACROSS →

1 Being well, being free from illness or disease

2 An injection

3 A small mass of living matter, the basic unit of each part of our body

4 Something taken to cure a disease or make a person more comfortable

5 A tame animal

6 To have fun in an activity or sport

7 To make muscles feel loose or less tense

8 An expression of thanks, as in "you're _____"

9 A group of people who are related

10 To travel on a boat moved by the wind

11 The food we eat three times a day

12 The red fluid that circulates in our veins

DOWN ↓

3 Abbreviation for computerized tomography

8 To have a desire for, to make a _____

13 Trust, the expectation that a wish will be granted

14 A place where sick and injured people are cared for

15 To find out and examine the value of something, such as blood

16 To provide with what is useful

17 A person trained to care for people who are sick

18 A powerful, invisible ray that can pass through solids to take a type of photograph

19 Peaceful, free from disturbance

20 A positive reply, the opposite of no

21 Abbreviation for intravenous

22 An area outside for playing

CROSSWORD PUZZLE CHALLENGE

Use these words for the puzzle:

blood, calm, cells, CT, family, healthy, help, hope, hospital
IV, meals, medicine, nurse, pet, play, relax, sail, shot
test, welcome, wish, xray, yard, yes,

Find the Hidden Alligators

As you color the picture look for the alligators lying quietly in the swamp.

How many hidden alligators can you find? ___

Peaceful Swamp

An alligator is able to lie so still that others visiting the swamp do not notice it. Draw the scene that the alligator sees as it rests quietly.

"I am comfortable as I lie quiet and still."

During scans, examinations, and treatments you can pretend to be an alligator and think about lying peacefully and quietly on the treatment table, just as an alligator lies quietly in a swamp.

Paintbrush Magic

Make a design all over the page using swirly lines. Color or paint the spaces using your favorite colors. When you are done, your picture may look like a stained glass window.

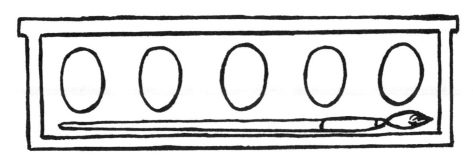

"I can brush away pain."

If you have uncomfortable feelings in your body you can send messages to your brain that will help you focus on more comfortable feelings. Pretend to use a magic paintbrush on your skin at times when you would like to brush on comfort and brush away pain.

~ Connect the Dots Game ~

Take turns. Draw a line between 2 dots either up or down or sideways anywhere on the paper. Your goal is to make a square by adding the last line that connects all four sides. You can build on any lines that are added by another player. As a square is made, the player who makes the last line claims it by writing his or her initials in it. When all the dots are used, the player with the most squares wins.

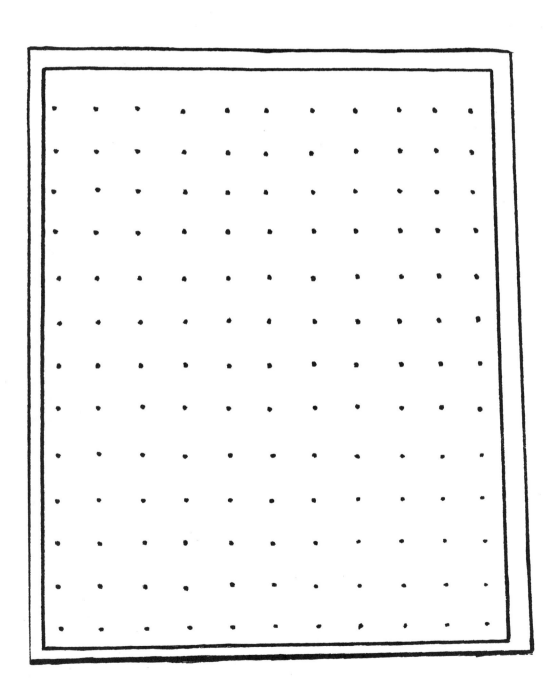

Jokes and Riddles

When we share a laugh with someone it makes us both feel better. Share these jokes and riddles with friends and see if you can bring a smile to their faces. Ask them to add to your collection. Share good feelings!

"Why do windows scream?"
"Because they have panes."

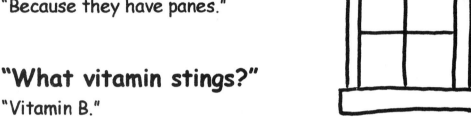

"What vitamin stings?"
"Vitamin B."

"What is the best thing to take before going swimming?"
"A deep breath."

"What's at the end of the rainbow?"
"The letter w."

"If you threw a brown rock into the Red Sea, what would it become?"
"Wet."

"What did one shelf say to the other shelf?"
"Boy, do you ever look board!"

"When is a piece of wood like a king?"
"When it's a ruler."

"What is in the middle of Texas?"
"X"

"What roof is always wet?"
"The roof of your mouth."

"What did the mommy lightning bug say to the daddy lightning bug?"
"Our baby certainly is bright!"

Why are letter A's like flowers?
Because B's come after them!

How are a doorbell and a bee alike?
They're both buzzers!

Add more jokes and riddles to your collection!

~ Soccer Victory ~
An active imagination "read-aloud" story

This is a story about the healthy cells in your body working together as your teammates to be winners against disease. Drops of medicine are compared to soccer balls.

Make a picture in your mind of a large, grassy soccer field. Breathe deeply and smell the fresh grass. The crisp air fills your lungs and gives you energy. Notice the colors around you; the green grass, bright uniforms, white clouds. Watch the gentle clouds moving across the sky. The gentle movement helps your breathing stay slow and relaxed.

You are ready to play a game of soccer. You have very special teammates in today's game. Your teammates are the millions of healthy cells that travel throughout your body. The soccer field is filled with your healthy cells that are ready to help you win your game.

What a great game this will be!

The ref blows the whistle to start the game. This is no ordinary game of soccer! Imagine that each drop of your medicine is a soccer ball that moves through your body. Your cells move the balls forward with incredible skill. They can spin and dodge and head the balls. They can dribble with amazing speed and control. They are all aiming for a special goal – your goal of being healthy.

Say to yourself three times, **"My whole body works to help me be strong and healthy."** Make a picture in your mind of kicking your medicine into the goal to defeat disease.

Imagine any unhealthy cells all clustered together inside the goal net. The unhealthy cells are confused. They do not spread out as your healthy cells do. They clump together. They make easy targets.

A ball of medicine soars off a teammate's foot, passes the goalie, and zooms into the net. Player after player aims a strong kick to the net. Player after player scores.

Your team destroys the unhealthy cells. What a game! It is a great feeling to take medicine that helps your body win against disease.

When you are ready to return to the room, take a deep breath. As you breathe out, open your eyes and stretch. You feel refreshed and relaxed. A strong team surrounds you whenever you take medicine.

~ SOCCER VICTORY ~

Start Here

(Directions on back)

Play a Game with a Partner

Directions for ~ *SOCCER VICTORY* ~

You need: 2 players

1 coin to use as the game piece (soccer ball)

You might want to cut the game page out of the book and place the game on a flat surface. A lunch tray or box top works well because your game piece will not escape.

The goal: To get the game piece into the net and score a point.

How to play: Decide how many total points you will need to win. (This will depend on how long you want to keep playing.)

Place the game piece (coin) in the *Start Here* box.

Choose player #1 and player #2.

Players take turns trying to get the game piece into the net.

Rules: Player #1 flicks the game piece with a finger.

Wherever the game piece (coin) lands, the next player takes his or her turn from the spot where the coin landed.

However:

~If the game piece lands in the net, player #1 scores 1 point and player #2 begins from the *Start Here* box.

~If the game piece lands out of bounds (beyond the net, or in the bleachers, or off the game board) then it is player #2 's turn. He or she gets to take a free kick by placing the game piece in the circle in the middle of the field.

~If a player's game piece lands on a *Germ*, that player takes another turn from that spot.

"My whole body works to help me be strong and healthy."

Think about the healthy cells in your body working as teammates to be winners against disease.

Try a Tangram

The word tangram means "Chinese drawing."
There are seven shapes in a tangram that can be used to create pictures and designs. All seven shapes must be used in a picture. Shapes may not overlap and must touch, if only at a single point.
   More than 300 pictures are possible. How many can you discover?

✂ Cut out the shapes below and have fun!
Want to match wits with a partner? To make more sets, put sheets of colored paper under this page and cut through all the pieces of paper.
(Hint: Save the pieces in an envelope so you can use them again.)

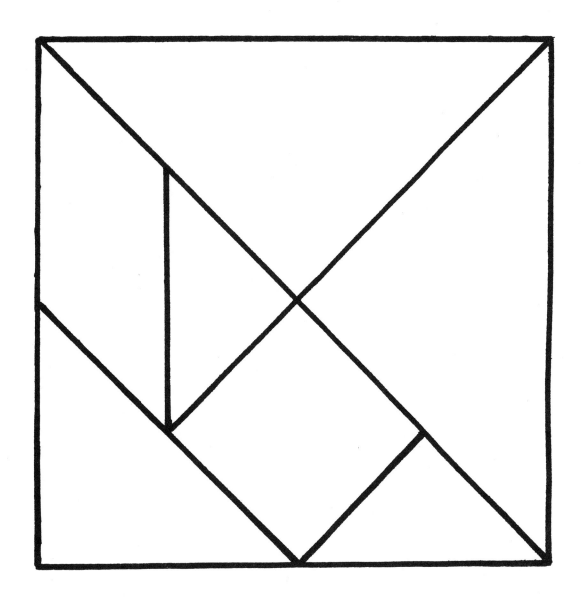

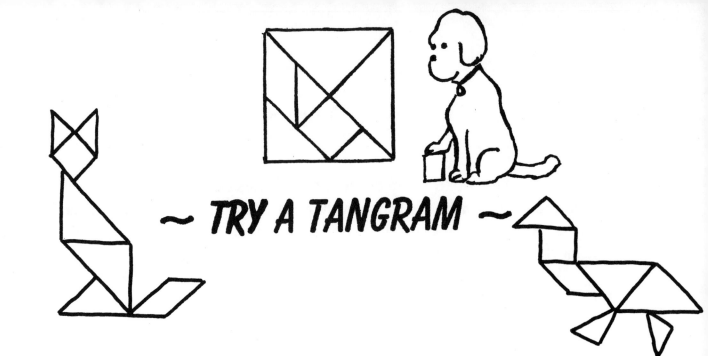

~ TRY A TANGRAM ~

Remote Control TV

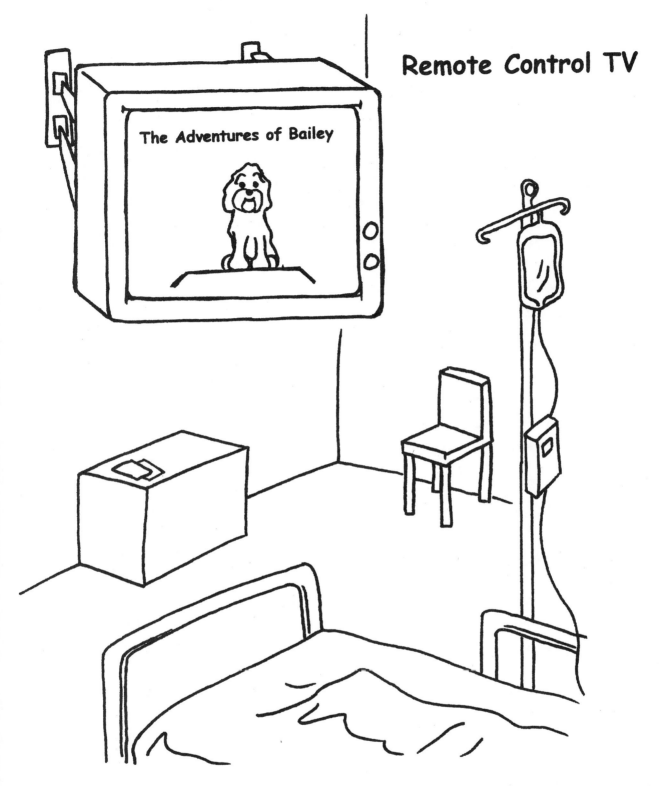

The Adventures of Bailey

"I can create peaceful, happy and relaxed feelings."

Each of us has a wide-range of emotions. Throughout each day our moods change. There are times in our lives when we can help ourselves feel better by changing how we feel about something.

~ Remote Control ~
An active imagination "read-aloud" story

In this story, you will pretend to use a remote control, not for your TV, but for your emotions. Imagine that you find a magical TV remote control. You are surprised to discover colorful writing on the back of it. The writing says, *"There are times in our lives when we can help ourselves feel better by changing how we feel about something."* That sounds interesting and you decide to give it a try. Before you do, take a deep breath to relax. As you breathe out, let your arms and legs get comfortable. Now you are ready to give your magical remote control a try. Push the button and slowly scan through your channels. What a surprise! Instead of seeing TV programs, you see stories from your own life! You discover a different story on each channel.

Flip through the channels and find one with a story that matches the way you are feeling right now. Think about how you are feeling. Imagine your TV screen showing that picture. Add details to the picture. Think about where you are. Name some of the things that you can see, touch, and smell in your very own show. **Enjoy your show!**

When you are ready to go to a different channel, take a deep breath. Blow the air out softly and slowly through your lips, then change to Channel #1 on your TV. Channel #1 is your Peaceful Channel. Picture yourself at a time when you felt peaceful. Think about what you see and what you hear. Think about what brings you happiness and relaxation in your life. Enjoy watching this peaceful show. Whenever you choose, you can switch to Peaceful Channel #1 and enjoy your peaceful feelings.

With your inner voice, repeat three times: **"I can create peaceful, happy, relaxed feelings."** You can choose one of your channels with comfortable, positive feelings whenever you wish.

When you change channels, remember that all your other feelings are still with you. You may have painful, or sad, or mad feelings. They are important too. Thinking about using your very own remote control helps you experience all your feelings.

When you feel ready to return to the room, take a deep breath. As you breathe out, open your eyes, and continue to enjoy your calm feelings.

The Adventures of

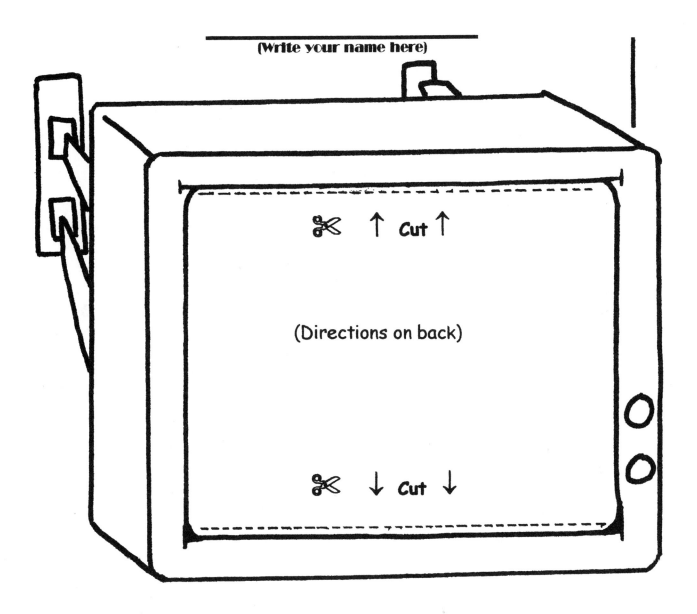

✂ ↑ Cut ↑

(Directions on back)

✂ ↓ Cut ↓

Thinking about using your own remote control helps you experience all of your feelings.

Whenever you wish, you can choose one of your channels showing your calm, comfortable, positive feelings.
Can you think of other times when your magical remote control would be helpful? For example, if you ever have an upset stomach you can make up a show that helps you feel better.

Directions for Your Remote Control TV

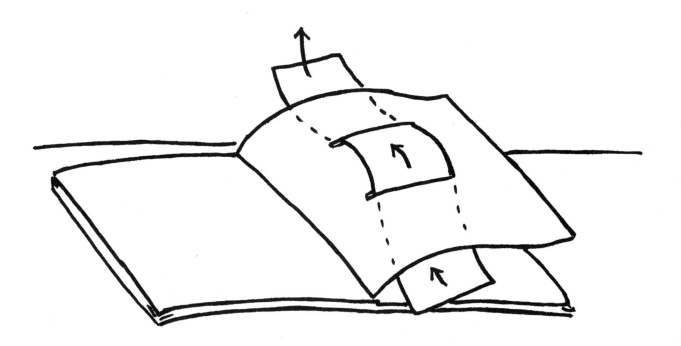

Cut out the TV screen strips on the next page. (Do not cut apart boxes.) Draw pictures in the boxes that tell a story of an event in your life and the way you were feeling at the time.

When you are ready to watch your show, cut slits on the TV screen where indicated.

Insert the top of your TV show strip in the bottom slit from the back of the page. Pull it up a bit over the page, then insert the strip into the top slit. Pull the paper strip through the slits to display your show.

Change the channel by putting in a new picture.

Remote Control TV Screens

✂ Cut the strips out of the book. Design your pictures. You can make extra strips from plain paper. Tape the strips together to make a longer show.

✂ ↓ Cut ↓

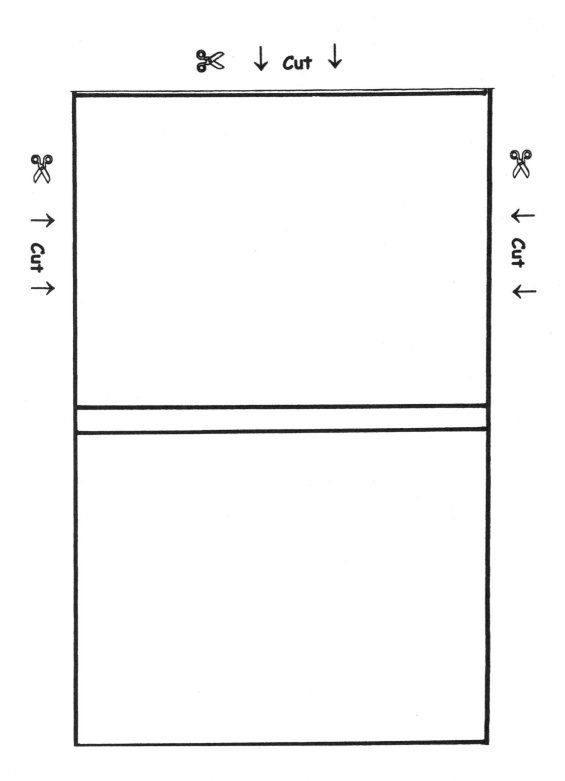

~REMOTE CONTROL TV~

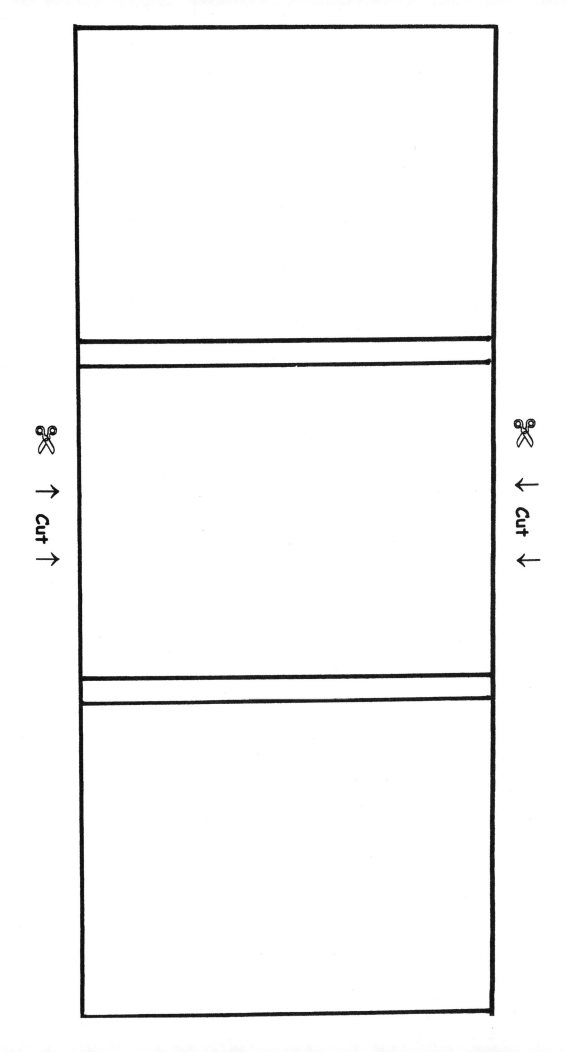

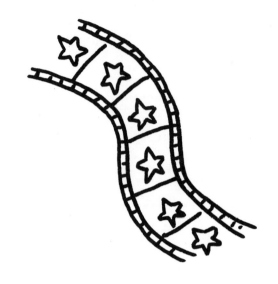

~REMOTE CONTROL TV~

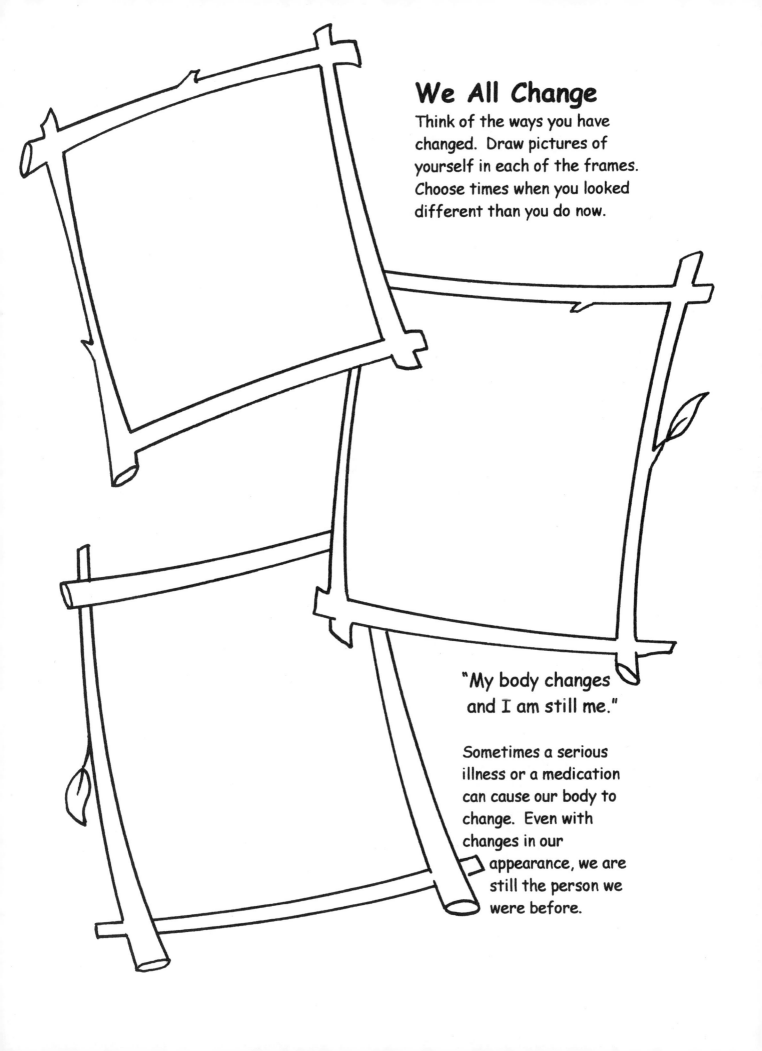

We All Change

Think of the ways you have changed. Draw pictures of yourself in each of the frames. Choose times when you looked different than you do now.

"My body changes and I am still me."

Sometimes a serious illness or a medication can cause our body to change. Even with changes in our appearance, we are still the person we were before.

✳ Snowflakes ✳

 Each one beautiful ~ Each one unique

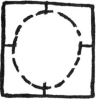

Design your own snowflakes by following these directions.

✂ Cut out the circle on the next page, OR use a coffee filter for your circle.

Fold the circle in half. Now fold it in half again.

Next, fold it into thirds. You will have formed a triangle, or cone shape.

✂ Cut notches of different sizes and shapes in the sides, top, and tip of the folded circle.

Open up the folded paper.

You have designed your own unique snowflake!

Make more snowflakes.

Put several snowflakes on string and attach them to a hanger to make a mobile to hang above your bed to look at as a focal point.

Put snowflakes on your window or wall.

When you look at your snowflakes think of this positive message:

"Healing is happening inside my body."

✷ Snowflakes ❋

❋ Each one beautiful ~ Each one unique ❋

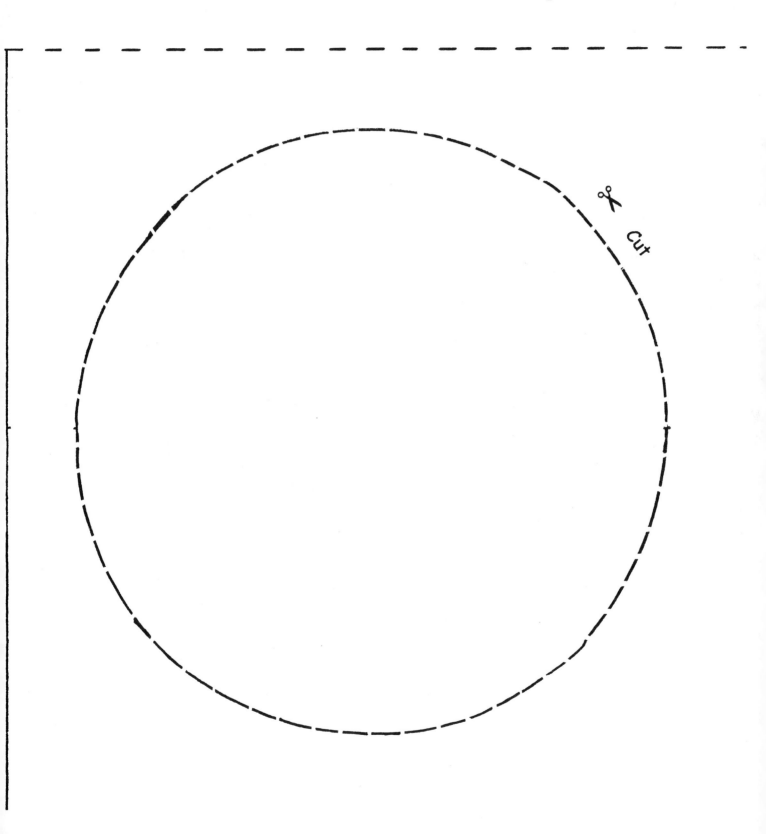

✂ Cut

Make a Card for Someone Special

Thinking of you

KEEP iN TOuCH

How are you?

What's new?

I miss you

✂ Cut along this line as well as along the side of this page. Fold the paper in half. Color a picture on the front. Write a message inside. Send it to your friend.

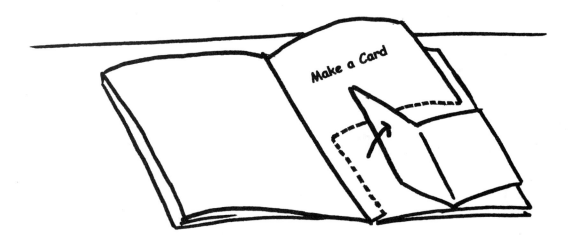

Stores have racks filled with get-well cards, thinking-of-you cards, birthday cards, holiday cards, thank you cards, and cards for almost any other occasion that you can imagine. People love to receive cards.

Can you think of a special event in a person's life? You can make more cards using blank paper. Sometimes card designers make cards that are cut into shapes. Try to make cut-out cards using your very own designs.

Keep in Touch with Special People

Name_____

Address_____

_____

Phone_____

Email_____

Name_____

Address_____

_____

Phone_____

Email_____

Name_____

Address_____

_____

Phone_____

Email_____

Name_____

Address_____

_____

Phone_____

Email_____

Plan Ahead

It's nice to know what to expect in the future. Fill in a calendar
with upcoming events and appointments.
Jot down things to do and questions that you would like to ask.

Sunday:

Monday:

Tuesday:

Wednesday:

Thursday:

Friday:

Saturday:

"Each day of treatment helps me become healthier."

A Dog-gone Good Word Search

Can you find these words?   Hint: Look in all directions!

```
x g w s k c k c h s
j y i b d k s f o v r
w c t n d y s m i l e s p
t x s i m a g i n e w z m
b q f p a b e l i e v e h k
m w n e r p x m e c a e p p
h d s t a r s y r s u n c y
z x s t c f r i e n d f z
k s g a m e l y w v x
z m h y d g z a r b g h
s j y g h g r b l l f t p m
a n c k i s n e l p g v b k
v c g j l u t a k d o l p
p t r a n u f g m o p r
j d p r e l a x m k l e f v
y t h e e n d c u b y e !
G o o d l u c k !  B a i l e y
```

Bailey

smiles

stars

fun

giggle

relax

dream

imagine

friend

game

play

believe

sun

peace

win

pets

the end bye!

ace ad age am arc are arm
cad cage came car care cram cream
dam dame dare dear deem
deer drag dream eager edge
era gear germ
grace grad grade gram greed
mad made mare me meager
merge race rad
rage ram read red reed
Did you find any others?

Bailey, Shadow, Waldo, and Sammy had x-rays taken. Draw lines to help the doctor match each dog to the correct x-ray. Then color the dogs.

x g w s k c k c h s
j y j b d k s f o v r
w c t n d y smile p
t x s imagine w z m
b q f p believe h k
m w n e r p x m e race p p
h d stars y r sun c y
z x s t c friend f z
k s game l y w v x
z m h y d g z a r b g h
s j y g h g r b l f t p m
a n c k j s n e l p g v b k
v c g j l u t a k d o l p
p t r a n u f g m o p r
j d p relax m k l e f v
y the end cu bye l
Good luck! Bailey

Bailey's Amazing Adventure

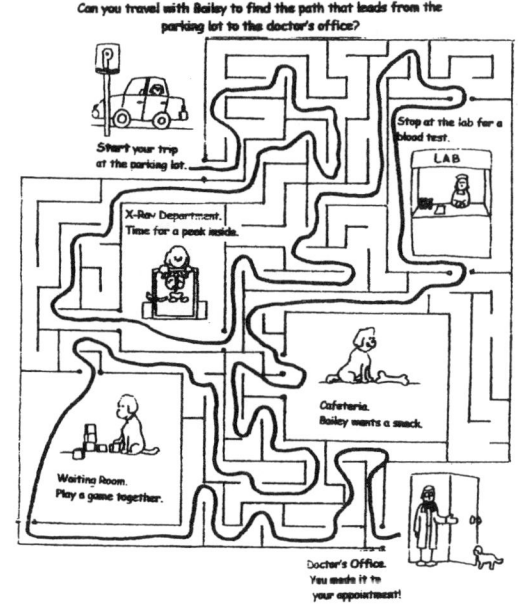

Can you travel with Bailey to find the path that leads from the parking lot to the doctor's office?

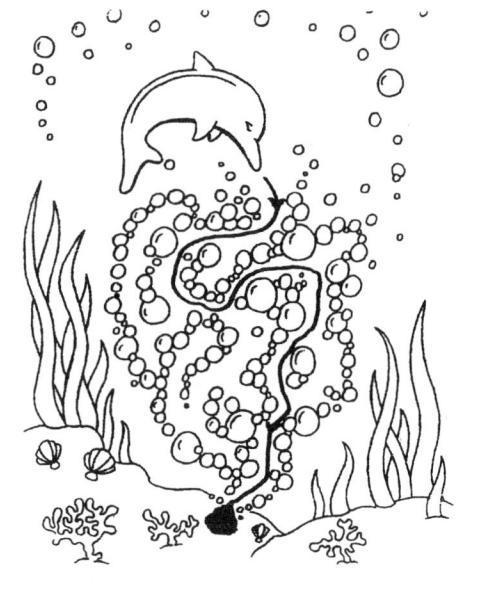

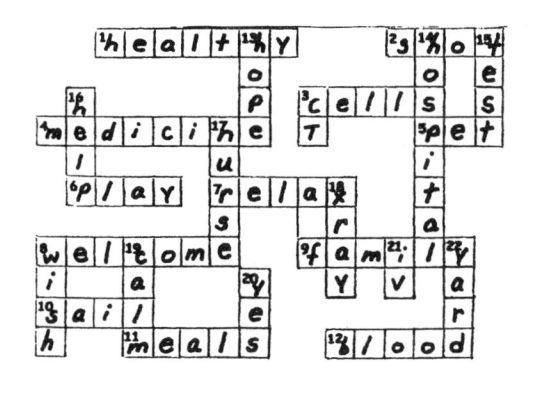

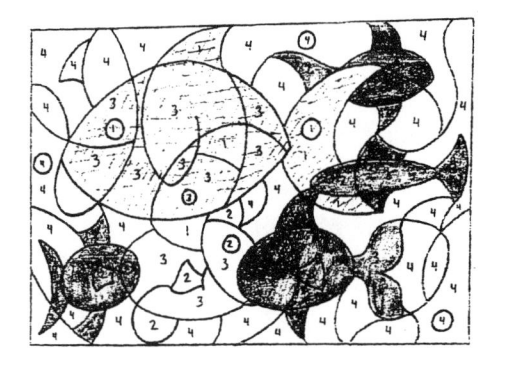

Note to Parents and Therapists

In the course of recovery and recuperation from an illness, children who have missed school and/or opportunities to play may need to strengthen muscles and remediate cognitive skills. Therapy for children is often accomplished through play. The activities in this booklet have been designed to foster therapeutic applications while your child is having fun. Therapists working with your child may wish to extend these activities with specific recommendations for ways to use these pages.

The following recommendations are suggestions by Sara Clark, M.S, OTR., Occupational Therapist, as examples of skills that may be reinforced within the Activity Book.

Eye-Hand Coordination and Fine Motor Coordination

Fine motor skills are those that require small muscle functioning, using muscles of the eyes, hands, and fingers. These skills are of particular importance to play and academic performance since they are necessary for handwriting, tool manipulation (such as cutting with scissors), and perceptual motor functioning such as scanning a page during reading, or copying from a blackboard.

- Flick a coin (Soccer Victory)
- Cutting (Snowflakes, Remote Control TV, Make a Card, Tangrams)
- Coloring designs (Giggle Wiggles, Field of Flowers)

Cognition (Thinking Skills)

- Color by number (Find the Fish, A Treat for Bailey)
- Crossword puzzles
- What does not belong?
- Make new words (Arcade Game)
- Word search

Visual-Motor Integration

Visual-motor integration is the process by which visual perception, how we perceive what we see, is integrated with a motor response such as when copying a design or figure.

- Draw Bailey (Now You Try)
- Color between the lines (numerous pages)
- Mazes (Dolphin, Amazing Adventure, Putting Out Fires, Follow the Lines)
- Connect the dots (The Settlers)
- Cutting (see above)

Visual Perception

Visual perception is assessed without the motor component. The components of visual perception include visual discrimination (perceiving differences in shapes), visual memory (remembering what was seen), visual form constancy (recognizing a familiar shape of varying size, color, orientation, etc.), visual sequential memory (remembering what was seen in proper sequence), figure ground (picking relevant visual information from a competing backround), and visual closure (seeing part of a shape and being able to mentally complete it).

- Matching shapes (Dogs and X-Rays, Turtle's Shell)
- Find the hidden fish
- Find the hidden alligators

Self-Expression

- Draw yourself, your friends
- Express your feelings (Dragon, Hospital Bracelet, Follow the Rainbow, Pleasant Dreams, Star Light)
- Writing in journal

Hand Strengthening

There are numerous small muscles in each hand. During extended hospital stays, children with chronic illnesses often receive medications through IV lines in their arms. When a child has an IV line in his/her arm, the child tends to use that arm and hand less and the hand muscles for functional activities are weakened.

- Molding rainbow clay
- Handwriting with pencils, markers, or crayons

With fond appreciation to my "review committee" who helped me fine-tune the fun:
Olivia Grych, Ryan Grych, Alison Schmidt, Kelsey Schmidt, Kevin Schmidt, Derek Schmidt, Heidi Schmidt, and special thanks to Krista Schmidt who designed the Secret Message page.

About Bailey:

Bailey was born in March, 1999. Bailey's mother was a cocker spaniel and Bailey's father was a poodle, so Bailey is a cockapoo. Bailey helped in the making of this book by jumping on my lap when I was working at the computer and jumping on my papers when I was writing. Mostly, Bailey helped me by being so cute and lovable.

About the Author:

Nancy Klein is a creative teacher who loves to challenge children to do their very best. She knows what it is like to be sick and to be in the hospital because she has had cancer two times. She has two children who are grown-up and live away from home. She and her husband live in Wisconsin and love to travel to warm beaches during the winter.

About the Artist:

Matt Holden has been drawing cool pictures since he was little. He loved to draw pictures of men fighting monsters. Matt knows what it is like to be sick and to be in the hospital because he had cancer when he was 12 years old. Now Matt is in an art major in college and he is studying animation.

Healing Images for Children Resources

Healing Images for Children:
Teaching Relaxation and Guided Imagery to Children Facing Cancer and Other Serious Illnesses
Written by Nancy C. Klein, M.A., Illustrated by Matthew Holden

A comprehensive guide for parents, health care providers, and other caring individuals complete with educational information relating to medical treatments and relaxation strategies. The first section of the book is written for adults and provides background information on research describing the healing power of relaxation, music, imagery, and humor. The second section includes chapters designed specifically to help children develop coping strategies to reduce the pain and anxiety of medical procedures and treatments. Twenty-seven stories help children reframe the medical and emotional aspects of illness with positive statements that reinforce one's ability to cope with difficulties. The guide is beautifully illustrated. A valuable adjunct to traditional medical interventions.
280 pages / 7 x 10 Softcover / ISBN 0-9636027-2-1

Healing Images for Children Activity Book:
Coloring/Drawing/Playing/Writing
For Days When Quiet Activities are Best
Written by Nancy C. Klein, M.A., Illustrated by Matthew Holden

A playful puppy, named Bailey, encourages children to express themselves and make this book their own through the exciting activities in this interactive workbook. Coloring, drawing, playing, and writing activities reinforce the themes of the active imagination stories and the positive messages regarding confidence, courage, and comfort. The individual activities are at several levels of difficulty appropriate for children ranging in age from 4 to 12+ years old. The book gives a sense of peace and well being along with encouragement and self-help ideas for any child coping with illness and/or hospitalization.
100 pages / 8.5 x 11 Softcover / ISBN 0-9636027-4-8

Healing Images for Children: Relax and Imagine CD
Written by Nancy C. Klein, Narrated by Roger Klein

Seven stories and a progressive muscle relaxation exercise are set to a background of calming music. The CD is a convenient, helpful way to reinforce the relaxation, breathing, and active imagination techniques from the book *Healing Images for Children*. It provides ready access to the calming messages from the book. Children can use the CD on the way to appointments, in waiting rooms, as well as during therapy.

70-minute audio recording / ISBN 0-9636027-3-X

Healing Images for Children Note Cards

Eight blank greeting cards each with a different picture representing a theme from an active imagination story in *Healing Images for Children*. The cards may be used as focal points to help children concentrate during difficult times or during relaxation exercises. Children may wish to write their own stories and positive messages inside the cards. The cards can be used to send encouragement to a loved one. (Includes envelopes)

Healing Images for Children Relaxation Kit
Activities to Bring Comfort ~ Toys to Bring Joy
Design and Guidebook by Nancy C. Klein, M.A.

Delightful activities chosen specifically to help a child remember the qualities from the active imagination stories in Healing Images for Children. Includes hands-on toys that can be tucked into a pocket and carried into waiting rooms, treatments, and diagnostic tests. Included are creative crafts, toys, stickers, and objects that stimulate personal interpretations of the stories and help children anchor their personal healing images. The components can be used therapeutically to encourage physical as well as emotional expression. All items are packaged in a carrying bag with handles. A guidebook with suggestions for use is included.
ISBN 0-9636027-5-6
   (Includes items not recommended for children under 3 years of age.)

Relaxation and Success Imagery Tape

(Klein & Klein) - A recording of the progressive muscle relaxation exercise as printed in the book *Healing Images for Children* including positive self-statements. Suitable for teens and adults. Original guitar background music. Available on tape.

Music for Relaxation, Learning, and Therapy

Studies show that music can reduce pain, unlock creativity, ease depression, and improve behavior. The following tapes/CDs are recommended and available through **Inner Coaching**.

Pianoscapes (Michael Jones) – Soothing piano solos.
Language of Love (Gary Lamb) – Relaxing music for classrooms, offices, or hospitals.
Pachelbel w/Ocean (Liv & Let Liv) – Cannon in D soundscape with three variations.
Bach Forever by the Sea (Dan Gibson) –Ten classics with sounds of the sea.
The Fairy Ring (Mike Rowland) – Calming music on piano/synthesizer.

Additional Resources from Inner Coaching

Ready...Set...R.E.L.A.X.
Written by Jeffrey S. Allen, M.Ed. and Roger J. Klein, Psy.D.

Beyond reviewing the causes of stress, this book equips children ages 5 to 13 years old with tools to overcome anxiety through the use of music, muscle relaxation, and storytelling to promote learning, imagination, and self-esteem. This fully researched program is used across the country by teachers, counselors, parents, and medical professionals as a preventive tool and intervention strategy. The 66 scripts focus on the following themes: R=Releasing Tension; E=Enjoying Life; L=Learning; A=Appreciating Others; X=X-panding Your Knowledge. Easy to use. Includes follow-up activities. 204 pages / 8.5 x 11 softcover / ISBN 0-9636027-0-5

Ready...Set...Release
Written by Jeffrey S. Allen, M.Ed. and Roger J. Klein, Psy.D.

This 74-minute cassette tape or audio CD offers 14 fun and calming exercises using music, breathing, muscle relaxation, and guided active imagination to soothe and release tension. This companion (or stand alone) piece to the book Ready...Set...R.E.L.A.X. has proven effective for children from preschool to middle school. ISBN 0-9636027-1-3

ORDER FORM

To order any of the resources listed below fill out this form and mail check and order form to:

Inner Coaching, 1108 Western Blvd, Watertown, WI 53094
FAX Purchase Orders to: 920/261-8801

QTY	ITEM	PRICE	TOTAL
_____	Healing Images for Children	$24.95	_____
_____	Healing Images for Children CD	$15.95	_____
_____	Healing Images Activity Book	$12.95	_____
_____	*Special package: above 3 items*	*$47.95*	_____
_____	Healing Images Relaxation Kit	$29.95	_____
_____	Healing Images Note Cards	$12.00	_____
_____	Ready…Set…R.E.L.A.X.	$23.95	_____
_____	Ready, Set, Release tape/CD	$ 10.95/15.95	_____
_____	Relaxation & Success Imagery	$10.95	_____
	MUSIC SELECTIONS	TAPE/CD	
_____	Pianoscapes	$10.95/15.95	_____
_____	Language of Love	$10.95/15.95	_____
_____	Pachelbel w/Ocean	$10.95/15.95	_____
_____	Bach Forever by the Sea	$10.95/15.95	_____
_____	The Fairy Ring	$10.95/15.95	_____

*Add $3.50 for first item and $.50 each additional item.   **SHIPPING***   _____

WI Residents add: 5.5% **Sales Tax**   _____

TOTAL   _____

Orders must be accompanied by check or money order made payable to Inner Coaching. Guaranteed – return within 30 days for refund if dissatisfied.

SHIP TO:
NAME:_____

ADDRESS:_____

_____

_____

PHONE:_____

E-MAIL:_____